Contents

With thanks to the members of the North Walsham & District Community Archive, North Walsham & District Historical Society, Paul Damen, John Otway, Paul Cubitt & Hazel Fuller for their contributions to this project, and the people of North Walsham for their unfaltering enthusiasm for our past projects which enabled the production of this book.

See more old North Walsham photos online at **www.northwalshamarchive.co.uk** or on our facebook group at **https://www.facebook.com/groups/NorthWalshamArchive**

Produced by Wayne Beauchamp, North Walsham. web: www.waynebeauchamp.co.uk
Published by North Walsham & District Community Archive. ©2020
Printed by Barnwell Print, 20 Dunkirk, Aylsham, Norwich NR11 6SU. tel: 01263 732767

Foreword

This book does not attempt to be an exhaustive history of the town but to show off the amazing collection of photographs taken by Fred Mace (and some from his father, Charles Mace which have survived in Fred's own archives). Fred is responsible for thousands more photographs than we have included here but many were for specific projects or promotional material for businesses and organisations along with recording local people and events. This book is focused on the amazing record he made of the streets, buildings and businesses of the town from the 1950s to the 1980s.

It is, therefore, quite a random collection as Fred did not create this collection with a view to it being published as a book. We've stayed away from ambiguous photographs, images of people, products or events and have purely focused on a tour of the town through the photographs of Fred Mace.

We hope you enjoy this collection as much as we did when we first received it from the North Walsham Historical Society who stood as custodians for the collection for many years. We've also included additional photos added from various sources acquired by our group over the years.

Wayne Beauchamp
Chairman of the North Walsham
& District Community Archive

About Fred Mace

Charles Frederick 'Fred' Mace, was born in Liverpool on 1st February 1922 the only child of Charles Eric Mace, a clothing manufacturer warehouseman (originally from the North Walsham area) and Bertha Lilian Mace (nee McKenny). The family moved to 36 Vicarage Street, North Walsham in 1939 around the same time that Fred joined the RAF where he served for the duration of World War II.

Charles set up his own photography business in North Walsham soon after their return to the North Walsham area. Their Vicarage Street home was part of the old North Walsham Vicarage which gave its name to the street. It was a large, white, 3 storey end terrace with a spacious south facing back garden where many of Charles Mace's photographs were shot. Charles also had a shop at the top of North Walsham Market Place, currently the Break charity shop, where many photographs were displayed in the front window.

Fred's parents Bertha and Charles Mace

At the age of 22 Fred married 21year old Mollie Chambers. Together they had 3 sons: Trevor in 1946, Richard in 1950 and Douglas in 1953. The boys were heavily involved in the North Walsham scouts but unfortunately none of them followed their father into photography.

The family lived at 19 Station Road, next door to a little shop called I.E.W. Riches (popular with the residents of Millfield estate), opposite the main gate to the Paston School field (now the Victory Swim and Fitness Centre). Page 131 shows the I.E.W. Riches shop in different incarnations over the years with the wall of Fred's house just visible on the left.

Fred had set up his own photography business in 1946 at the age of 24. He was the seventh generation of his family to do so in the North Walsham area. Not just photographing portraits, children, weddings, etc but undertaking commercial and industrial projects too; it seems that everybody in the town from that time was either photographed by Fred or knows somebody who was. He was an Associate of The Master Photographers Association (AMPA), a qualification which denotes a high standard of craftsmanship and individual creative ability. Fred also became a freelance photographer for the North Norfolk News.

In his free time Fred was apparently an excellent table tennis player who coached at the North Walsham Youth Centre in Park Lane during the 1960s.

Fred's father, Charles, died in September 1973 and his mother, Bertha, died in November 1978.

In later life Fred and Mollie moved to 3 St Benets Avenue, North Walsham.

Fred Mace

Fred retired from photography in 1992 at the age of 70 after 46 years as a professional photographer saying "I have photographed three generations of some families' weddings. When they say they want a picture of grandad I know exactly who he is".

Fred died at the age of 86 on 24th October 2008 in his home town of North Walsham.

Equipment

Local photographer, Paul Damen, in 2003. At his left hand is Fred Mace's actual 5"x4" Linhof Technika which Paul now owns and was used by Fred Mace to photograph many of the lovely old photos in this book.

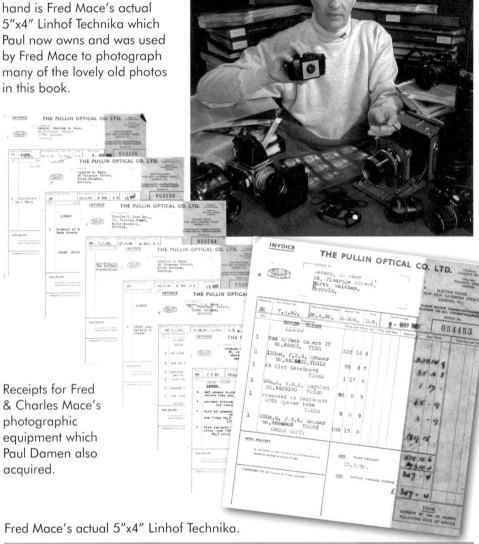

Paul Damen

Receipts for Fred & Charles Mace's photographic equipment which Paul Damen also acquired.

Fred Mace's actual 5"x4" Linhof Technika.

Personal memories of Fred

I worked in the drawing office at Crane Fruehauf in North Walsham from 1966 to 1972 alongside Pat Pipe, Tom Wade, Russell Bryant and others. I produced working drawings for flats, vans, containers and truck bodies as well as spares and sales manuals. I would regularly meet with Fred when he came to photograph mainly new completed products for Crane Fruehauf records and various publications. He was a little man (no offence!) with a big

John Otway

personality & a big sense of humour and was invariably coated in fag ash! We often discussed our mutual love of photography and he eventually persuaded me to assist him with wedding photography. His services were much in demand and for a few years I would be called upon to 'perform' in his place at weddings in and around North Walsham while he was also out doing weddings and various other assignments himself. He provided me with a list of photos that MUST be adhered to consisting of 12 colour photos and 36 plus black and white with details of the sequence of the shots, how to pose them, and who should appear in them - arriving at the church or registry office, inside during the ceremony and at the reception. I would then go back to his house in Station Road with the equipment for inspection and the rolls of film for him to develop. He produced black and white prints upstairs in his dark room and posted the colour films to be processed in Colchester. He would then call me mid week when processing was complete to discuss the results! I learned a lot from Fred during these discussions! I had some interesting experiences along the way such as Brides being very late, Brides' mums being VERY fussy, double bookings with other photographers, faulty equipment (very rare) and dodgy weather. Fred would listen sympathetically and very calmly to my tales of woe with reassurances that everything would

be OK and I would still get paid (not a lot!) Using black and white and colour 120 roll film with a variety of manual loading cameras was an art in itself and Fred was very particular as to the correct way to carry out these tricky tasks successfully. In short he was a perfectionist in his art!! These are some of the cameras and pieces of equipment provided by him - quite a weighty load! - There were always 2 cameras, 1 for colour and 1 for black and white: - Zeiss Super Ikonta with folding bellows in the beginning, then Rollieflex twin lens reflex and finally a new and very expensive Hasselblad single lens reflex. The flash equipment was a hand held gun with cables to connect to

the camera and to a very heavy battery charger around my neck and a very heavy ex war department wooden tripod! On one memorable occasion the tripod with a Hasselblad on top was blown over by an Easterly gale outside Happisburgh church: both still worked but turned out a bit worse for wear! Fred was a patient man and took it all in his stride! Fred was a kind, friendly man with a knack of making everyone he met feel at ease and important to him! I thoroughly enjoyed my years working with him!

John Otway

Charles Mace Photographic, Market Place.

North Walsham Produce Centre, Market Place.

Penelope & The Cross Keys Hotel, Market Place. 1950s.

Cross Keys Hotel, Market Place.

Fishing Tackle shop (The Cross Keys Hotel), Market Place.

In the 1980s the Cross Keys Hotel became Woolworth.

North Walsham through the lens of Fred Mace

The rear of The Cross Keys Hotel.

The rear of The Cross Keys Hotel.

The rear of The Cross Keys Hotel.

The rear of The Cross Keys Hotel.

North Walsham through the lens of Fred Mace

S. H. Sexton, Butcher, Market Place.

S. H. Sexton, Butcher, Market Place.

Currys and E. Underwood & Sons in the Market Place.

Hancock Jewellers in the Market Place (probably Charles Mace).

Maison Leslie, Market Place.

Labour Party outing departing from the Market Place.

R. W. Gyton, Market Place. 1956.

Midland Bank, Market Place.

North Walsham through the lens of Fred Mace

St Nicholas' Church.

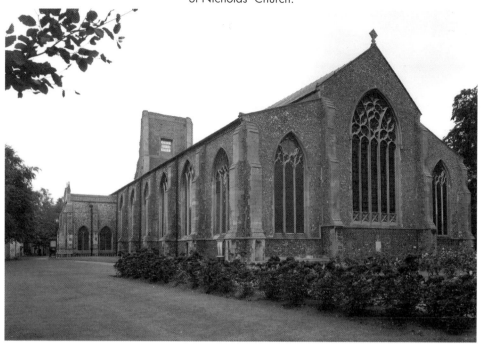

Inside St Nicholas' Church.

North Walsham through the lens of Fred Mace

North side of the Market Place.

North side of the Market Place.

North Walsham through the lens of Fred Mace

Black Horse Agencies, Market Place.

E. Underwood & Sons, Market Place. 1974.

R. Edmonds & Son, Market Place.

R. Edmonds & Son, Market Place.

North Walsham through the lens of Fred Mace

1927 Austin Windsor EX1938 outside Jeary's, Market Place.

1927 Austin Windsor EX1938 outside Ling's, Market Place.

North Walsham Market Place.

South side of the Market Place.

North Walsham Market Place.

North Walsham Market Place.

Stead & Simpson, Market Place.

Loads, Market Place.

North Walsham Market Cross.

North Walsham Market Cross.

Jarvis Bros. Fish Merchants, Market Street.

Blyth's Store, Market Street.

Market Street. c1960.

J. Hall, Florist, Market Street.

St Nicholas' Court Shopping Precinct.

St Nicholas' Court Shopping Precinct.

North Walsham through the lens of Fred Mace

St Nicholas' Court Shopping Precinct.

St Nicholas' Court Shopping Precinct.

Church Street.

Church Street.

North Walsham through the lens of Fred Mace

Rusts Ltd., Church Street.

Rusts Ltd., Church Street.

Church Street. 1960.

Church Street.

F. W. Woolworth & Co. Ltd., Church Street.

F. W. Woolworth & Co. Ltd., Church Street.

Kings Arms Street.

Lloyds Bank, Kings Arms Street.

Rear of Lloyds Bank, Kings Arms Street.

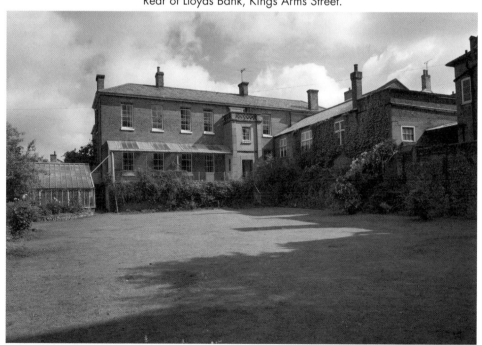

Kings Arms Street.

Kings Arms Street.

North Walsham through the lens of Fred Mace

Kings Arms Street.

Kings Arms Street. 9th February 1960.

Kings Arms Street / Park Lane. 9th February 1960.

Kings Arms Street / Park Lane. 9th February 1960.

Park Lane.

Park Lane.

Park Lane.

Park Lane.

Hall Lane. 1960.

Rear of cottages on Hall Lane. 1960.

North Walsham through the lens of Fred Mace

Hall Lane. 1960.

Hall Lane. 1960.

Rounce & Wortley Ltd Printers, Hall Lane.

Grove Road.

Grove Road.

North Walsham through the lens of Fred Mace

Kimberley Road.

Mitre Tavern Yard.

Bacton Road. 6th May 1960.

Bacton Road. 26th December 1959.

Bacton Road. 6th May 1960.

Bacton Road. 6th May 1960.

Bacton Road. 6th May 1960.

Hannants Garage Ltd on Bacton Road. 1969.

North Walsham through the lens of Fred Mace

Hannants Garage Ltd, Bacton Road.

Hannants Garage Ltd, Bacton Road.

Bacton Road. 26th December 1959.

Bacton Road. 6th May 1960.

Bacton Road.

Bacton Road. 6th May 1960.

Bacton Road / Reeves Court

Dog Yard. 3rd November 1960.

North Walsham through the lens of Fred Mace

Dog Yard. 3rd May 1960.

Dog Yard. 3rd November 1960.

Dog Yard. 3rd November 1960.

Dog Yard. 3rd November 1960.

Dog Yard. 3rd May 1960.

Dog Yard. 3rd November 1960.

Dog Yard. 3rd November 1960.

Dog Yard. 3rd November 1960.

North Walsham through the lens of Fred Mace

Dog Yard. 3rd May 1960.

Dog Yard. 3rd November 1960.

Dog Yard. 3rd May 1960.

Dog Yard. 3rd May 1960.

Dog Yard. 1965. (Vicarage Street in the background).

Entrance to Dog Yard from Bacton Road viewed from Vicarage Street.

H. Grey & Son General Stores, corner of Vicarage Street & Bacton Road. c1940.

Fundraising for the Merchant Navy on Vicarage Street. 1940s.

Vicarage Street.

Vicarage Street.

Vicarage Street.

Vicarage Street.

Vicarage Street.

Vicarage Street.

North Walsham through the lens of Fred Mace

Vicarage Street.

J. T. Hewitt, Saddler. Church Plain on Vicarage Street

B. Gunton, Butcher on North Street.

North Street.

North Walsham through the lens of Fred Mace

Entrance to Ship Yard from Church Plain.

Catspit Lane / Catchpit Lane (now Northfield Road).

North Walsham through the lens of Fred Mace

Catspit Lane / Catchpit Lane (now Northfield Road).

Catspit Lane / Catchpit Lane (now Northfield Road). 24th December 1959.

North Walsham through the lens of Fred Mace

Catspit Lane / Catchpit Lane (now Northfield Road).

Northfield Road.

Northfield Road.

Northfield Road.

North Walsham through the lens of Fred Mace

Northfield Road.

Northfield Road.

Gas Services Shop on Mundesley Road

Mundesley Road

Mundesley Road. June 1965.

Mundesley Road.

Mundesley Road.

Mundesley Road. 24th December 1959.

North Walsham through the lens of Fred Mace

Building Hadfield Road off Mundesley Road.

Building Hadfield Road off Mundesley Road.

Mundesley Road. 26th October 1959.

Mundesley Road. 26th October 1959.

Meadowview Stores, Mundesley Road.

Mundesley Road. 1964.

Lyngate Road. c1960.

East Coast Plastics, Folgate Road.

St Mary's Way under construction.

St Mary's Way under construction.

Happisburgh Road. c1960.

Happisburgh Road. c1960.

North Walsham through the lens of Fred Mace

Happisburgh Road. c1960.

Happisburgh Road. c1960.

Happisburgh Road. c1960.

North Walsham New High School, Spenser Avenue.

Spenser Avenue.

Spenser Avenue.

Spenser Avenue.

Spenser Avenue.

North Walsham through the lens of Fred Mace

Nigel F. Hedge office on Grammar School Road.

Wilkinson & Davies Solicitors on Grammar School Road. March 1977.

Grammar School Road.

Grammar School Road. 2nd July 1962.

Grammar School Road. 2nd July 1962.

Paston Grammar School.

Bank Loke.

Dewhurst's van in Bank Loke.

Bank Loke.

North Walsham through the lens of Fred Mace

Cottages on New Road.

Back of the cottages on New Road.

New Road.

North Walsham through the lens of Fred Mace

New Road.

Fire Station on New Road. 1960s.

North Walsham through the lens of Fred Mace

Fire Station on New Road. 1960s.

Fire Station on New Road. 1960s.

The old cattle market on Yarmouth Road.

The old cattle market on Yarmouth Road.

Post Office, Yarmouth Road.

Post Office, Yarmouth Road.

Yarmouth Road. 28th October 1960.

North Walsham through the lens of Fred Mace

Yarmouth Road.

Yarmouth Road. 28th October 1960.

The Oaks Restaurant on Yarmouth Road.

The Oaks Restaurant on Yarmouth Road. 28th October 1960.

Construction of Fine Fare, Yarmouth Road. Early 1980s.

Construction of Fine Fare, Yarmouth Road. Early 1980s.

Construction of Fine Fare, Yarmouth Road. Early 1980s.

Construction of Fine Fare, Yarmouth Road. Early 1980s.

The Oaks Lodge on Yarmouth Road being demolished. 28th October 1960.

Yarmouth Road.

Yarmouth Road. 16th April 1960.

Yarmouth Road. 16th April 1960.

Yarmouth Road.

Yarmouth Road.

Cottage Hospital entrance, Yarmouth Road.

Cottage Hospital entrance, Yarmouth Road.

Rose Meadow, Yarmouth Road.

LeGrice Nurseries, Yarmouth Road.

Yarmouth Road Gravel Pit.

Yarmouth Road Gravel Pit.

Hadfields Garden Centre, Yarmouth Road.

Hadfields Garden Centre, Yarmouth Road.

Scarborough Hill House, Yarmouth Road.

Norwich Road.

Harmer & Scott's Garage, Norwich Road.

Harmer & Scott's Garage, Norwich Road.

Bridge damage at Norwich Road.

North Walsham through the lens of Fred Mace

Norwich Road. January 1965.

Norwich Road. January 1965.

Norwich Road. January 1965.

Norwich Road. June 1966.

North Walsham through the lens of Fred Mace

Norwich Road. June 1966.

Norwich Road. June 1966.

Norwich Road. January 1965.

Norwich Road. January 1965.

Filming for H. P. Smedley, Norwich Road.

H. P. Smedley, Norwich Road.

H. P. Smedley, Norwich Road.

H. P. Smedley, Norwich Road.

North Walsham through the lens of Fred Mace

Construction of the cooling tower at H. P. Smedley, Norwich Road.

Ladbrook Manufacturing Ltd, Norwich Road.

Road works outside Monument Cottage, Norwich Road.

Cherry Tree Lane.

Cherry Tree Lane.

Bradfield Road. 9th June 1962.

Bradfield Road. 9th June 1962.

Bradfield Road.

Bradfield Road.

Bradfield Road.

Bradfield Road.

Bradfield Road.

Bradfield Road.

Cromer Road / Bradfield Road.

Cromer Road / Bradfield Road.

North Walsham through the lens of Fred Mace

Cromer Road / Cherry Tree Lane

Cromer Road / Cherry Tree Lane

Cromer Road / Cherry Tree Lane

Cromer Road.

Construction of Crane Fruehauf, Cromer Road.

Construction of Crane Fruehauf, Cromer Road.

Crane Fruehauf, Cromer Road.

Crane Fruehauf, Cromer Road.

Kingsway. 1959.

Kingsway. 1959.

Greens Road.

Greens Road.

North Walsham through the lens of Fred Mace

Top end of Station Road. June 1966.

Top end of Station Road. June 1966.

Top end of Station Road. June 1966.

Bottom end of Station Road.

Motique, Station Road.

Contrast Hairdressers, Station Road.

Field View (Millfield Estate).

Field View (Millfield Estate).

North Walsham through the lens of Fred Mace

Millfield Estate. 1962.

Millfield Estate. 1962.

Millfield Estate. 1962.

Millfield Estate. 1962.

Millfield Estate. 1962.

Millfield Estate. 1962.

Burton Avenue (Millfield Estate). 26th October 1959.

Oak Road. 9th June 1962.

North Walsham through the lens of Fred Mace

Oak Road. 9th June 1962.

Oak Road. 9th June 1962.

Skeyton New Road. 9th June 1962.

Skeyton Road.

Marshgate. c1960.

Marshgate. c1960.

Marshgate.

Marshgate.

Marshgate.

Marshgate.

Construction of the Bypass. 1976.

Construction of the Bypass. 1976.

Construction of the Bypass. 1976.

Construction of the Bypass. 1976.

The Granary at Briggate Mill, 1974.

Construction of Bacton Gas Terminal.

North Walsham through the lens of Fred Mace